COPYRIGHT

CASES

Anchita Sood

Daman Dev Sood

Front and back covers designed by -

Tanuj Sood

Student- Batchelor of technology (CSE), AKGEC Ghaziabad

Foreword

Daman Dev Sood continues his series of highly readable but serious books on topics relevant to Resilience with this, his fourth book, focused on copyrights. Without copyright, there can be no protection of intellectual property and little intellectual Resilience.

Plagiarism is theft and only copyright law protects authors and creative artists from wholesale theft of their intellectual property.

New books contain warnings about copyright and resale, but multiple resales take place without any payment of royalties, although the intellectual or entertainment value of the used book or work of art remains unchanged.

Daman, with Anchita Sood has made a good attempt in bringing this issue up and resolving some real cases.

Andrew Hiles
Founder - BCI, Professor Emeritus of BCM,
Telfort Business Institute, Shanghai University
Tiffany, France
June 2022

Contents

1. Background

Doctrine of Fair Dealing allows a person to use or produce copyright protected material of an individual/organization under certain circumstances so that the sanctity of the original work is not tarnished as well as the rights of the proprietor.

Globally, fair dealing was recognized a long time ago. However, in India, the scope of fair dealing is very limited and inadequate in comparison with international copyright law.

In this book, the authors have tried to analyse some cases and how they fall under the doctrine of fair use.

The objective of the book is to raise awareness and enhance resilience (personal – to be fair – to organizational – to global).

I recently came to know that India has a National IPR Policy (hence we begin with that as first case).

Where possible direct communication with the author(s) has been included. My questions are in black and the responses from various authorities/ departments/ persons are in purple.

REAL CASES BASED DISCUSSIONS PAPER

What does having COPYRIGHT mean?

Having a copyright means you have all the rights over that work, and no one can use that work without your due permission or without giving you the credits.

2. Case1: National (Indian) IPR Policy

I recently came across our National IPR Policy, downloaded it, read it, and had a question, so wrote this to the concerned department in the government:

"I have downloaded "http://cipam.gov.in/wp-content/uploads/2020/10/FINAL_FILE_National_IPR_Book_240616_EDITED_A.pdf" from your website. The document is freely available to all, does not have any copyright information. So, am I in infringement of any law by downloading and sharing this with other people? – Can you help by answering this question please?"

And a quick response (to my surprise – within 24 hours – we struggle to maintain this even in the big corporate houses). Not just response – like automated acknowledgement- it was full resolution:

"Thank you for writing to us. If a copyrighted work is used for educational or research purposes then it is considered fair use and not an infringement under

Indian Copyright Act, Section 52. Although, it is advisable to refer to and quote the work to avoid plagiarism."

My questioning continued:

"Little more please – this National IPR Policy that I downloaded from your website doesn't say anything about copyrights (I mean there is no © sign or any text about who holds the IPR on this document. So, if I use this even in my research or share with some other people – am I breaking any rule/ law?"

And a quick and affirmative (unlike our medical test reports from various labs – never conclusive – always end with 'recommended clinical correlation' or so):

"Copyright is an inherent right and comes into existence as soon as the work is created, the c sign is only indicative in nature. Since the National IPR policy is already in the public domain name if you share it with others, you would not be breaking the law."

Responding agency is Cell for IPR Promotion and Management (CIPAM)

Project Room - F

Udyog Bhawan

Rafi Ahmed Kidwai Marg

Delhi-110011

3. Case2: Bank of England's Governor's Speech

Bank of England's Governor recently delivered a speech available at <u>A resilient financial system - speech by Andrew Bailey | Bank of England</u> . My initial impression would be that this was 'publicly available information' hence no copyright violation in using and sharing this information. The page at the bottom does have '(@)2022 Bank of England'.

I still wrote to them "I am developing a course on Operational Resilience. Can I refer to the Governor's speech available at <u>A resilient financial system - speech by Andrew Bailey | Bank of England</u> ? I will not change any text and can give any other reference that you prefer. Please let me know."

Here is the response

"We are content to grant you non-exclusive rights to link to the Governor's recent speech, subject to acknowledgement of the source."

I had another question in mind (no one is perfect, I am a firm believer, but I would not like to make a mistake knowingly, so a further clarification to close the loop):

"I am sharing the document as pdf as downloaded using said button from your site and am saying that 'Governor, Bank of England's speech is available as downloadable resource' - hope this is ok."

And the concluding remark:

"Thank you for your further email.

This is fine, but please note, that it cannot be re-published publicly, and because these documents are subject to revision and correction, the version you store locally may become out of date."

Responding agency is Engagement & Enquiries Group | Communications

Bank of England | Threadneedle Street | London | EC2R 8AH

+44 (0)20 3461 4878

4. Case3: BCI GPG 2018

As a Fellow Member of the BCI, I recently got to download the GPG 2018 Addendum version. And here is my conversation with them:

"I am a member of the BCI (FBCI) and have just downloaded the above document (I believe nothing wrong in this so far).

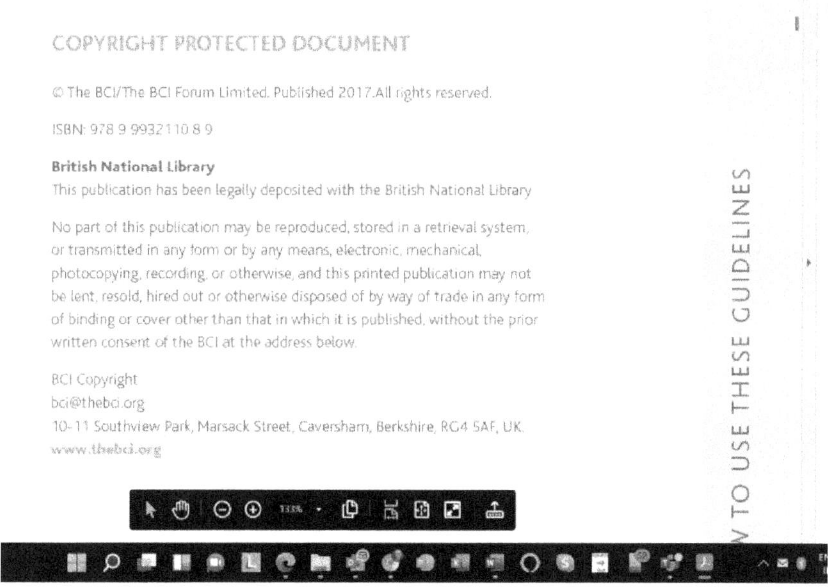

The copyright notice in the book says '..no part of this publication may be reproduced, **stored in a retrieval system**…' – so am I making a mistake by storing on my machine that is backed up on a regular basis, and I may make multiple copies of backup also? "

Please let me know, I want to be sure and make it part of my research on IPRs.

What is British National Library and what role does it play in protecting rights is to be discussed separately.

Quick response from the BCI:

"As a member you are allowed to keep your own personal copy of the GPG stored on your own machine. So please rest assured that you are doing nothing wrong ☺

The copyright notice referring to *'..no part of this publication may be reproduced, stored in a retrieval system…*' means that people are not allowed to store it on a company website, or system that can be accessed by lots of people within that organisation, without a special licence."

While my interpretation doesn't match with theirs, I am happy to continue.

The response came from **Customer Services Manager.**

5. Case4: IIA ONRISK 2022

The seeds for this case for sown due to a fact that we share a lot of information and documents social media groups. The following document (now showing page1 as I have the permission) called 'ONRISK 2022' produced by IIA in a whataspp professional group.

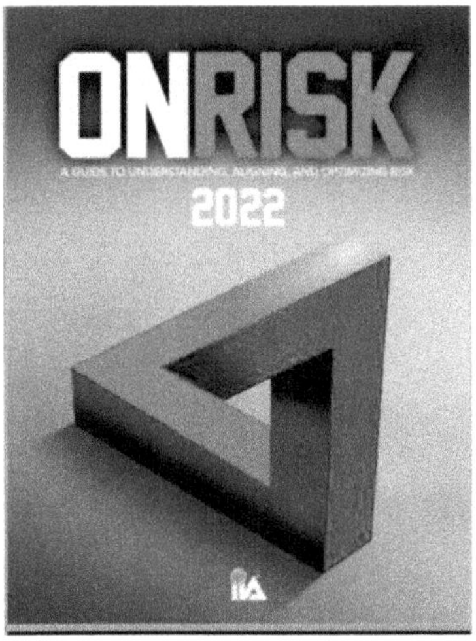

To resolve it, I wrote to someone I knew at IIA (hence I expected to get this resolved faster – either this way or that. So, the interaction started:

"Dear Nikhel

I received the above document through someone in a whatsapp group post today.

1. Is it appropriate?
2. I am presenting a webinar on Risks on 26th Feb and would like to make reference to the contents of this document – is there any restriction? "

First question perhaps never got clarified, but I reproduce the entire interaction (with his permission):

"Dear Daman,

My apologies for misunderstanding. I think ONRISK2022 is a public document available in the public domain. As long as you quote the source there should not be an issue. Unless the copyright provisions in the document (which I have not checked) state otherwise. Sorry that the date passed but I hope you can quote it in the future as well J. "

My response: "The document on the last page has this text:

"""""""

Copyright
Copyright © 2021 The Institute of Internal Auditors, Inc. All rights reserved. For permission to reproduce, please contact <u>copyright@theiia.org</u>.

"""""""

But I am not reproducing – rather just using some of the information. So, hope OK. But please let me know, I want to be sure, as I am developing some cases around IPR violations and would not like to break the law myself.

I wish to add one more question – as I received it from a professional contact (who posted in a whatsapp group), can I also distribute it further? No changes to be made – to be shared in original shape, size, logo etc.?"

I wrote to Nikhel further:

"Can I make reference to these discussions in my paper/ webinar etc.? I can mask your identity, if you wish, while the value will be in using it with your name, designation. "

"Since we have time I can try to get a clarification from IIA Global. Thanks for raising a point where I could do with some clarity myself.

My own understanding is that if we quote from an article verbatim technically one is supposed to get an approval from the Author/Institute as the case maybe. Practically most people just ascribe it to the source, and nothing happens in practice. If you draw conclusions and create your own material from documents in the public domain there is no issue at all.

However will revert after I receive a response. "

This actually resolved many queries that I had (cases coming up later).

IIA responded further:

"Anyone using/ reproducing materials / content from The IIA should give proper credit in writing or verbal to the original source."

The interaction was with
Nikhel Kochhar
Chief Advisor
The IIA India
ceo@iiaindia.co
www.iiaindia.co

I reproduce the case with his credentials with his permission.

And the webinar 'The Art of Managing Risks Effectively in 2022' was successfully delivered on 26th Feb with reference to IIA ONRISK2022 Report as desired by the authors. The recording is available at https://www.youtube.com/watch?v=VyaQjGB2E7Q .

There are few more cases in this category, where I wish to use publicly available information/ document (without any changes and with due reference to the source) – have written to the owner organizations, but there is no response. I am moving ahead 'no response means they do not have any challenge'. I am clear in seeking clarity. Not sure whether this approach is legally correct/ acceptable.

6. Case5: NarayanaHealth website

Publicly available information: have a look at
https://www.narayanahealth.org/ .

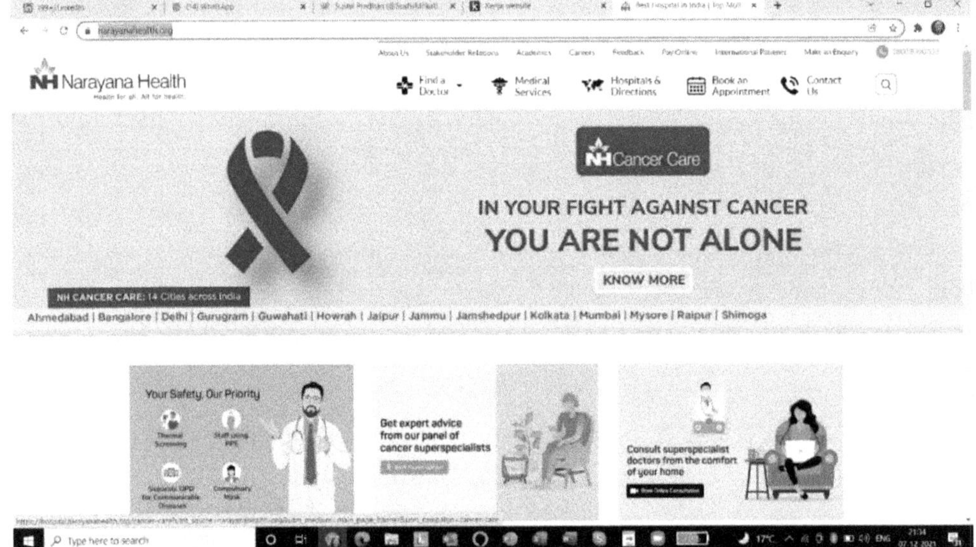

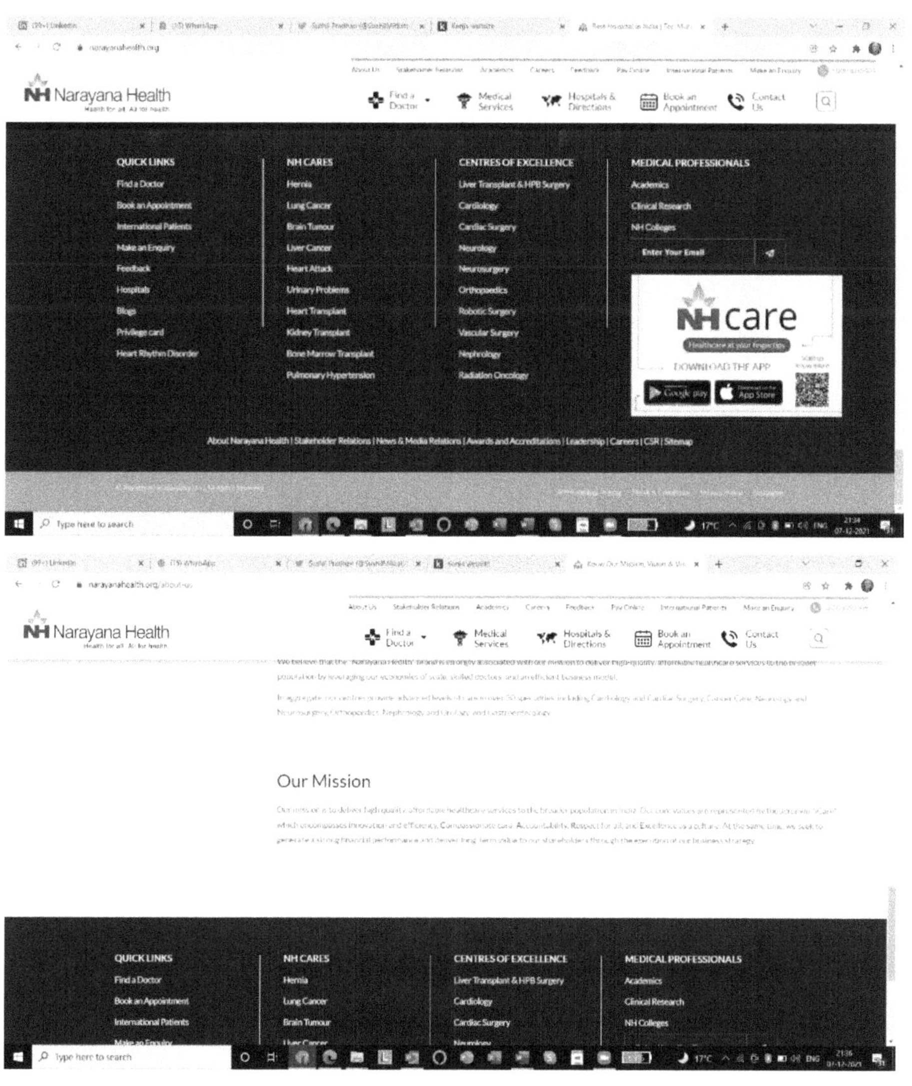

At the bottom it says © Narayana Hrudayalaya Ltd | All Rights Reserved

I pick up this 'Our Mission' information and use in one of my papers.

I believe this is 'publicly available information' and can be freely used (I have not made any changes and have given reference of the site also). Am I infringing any rule/ regulation/ act?

What does the 'copyright' at the bottom of the page mean?

Commentary:

In the present case, we can see that the user is asking to use information that is available on the website of a hospital and on the bottom of the webpage the term "ALL RIGHTS RESERVED" is written.

The use of words "ALL RIGHTS RESERVED" means that no one may utilise your work without first getting permission from you. This declaration is not required by law, therefore omitting it will have no legal consequences. The statement is redundant because people cannot utilise copyrighted works without permission from the copyright holder.

But the Copyright Act of 1957 provides for exceptional cases where the using of work without the consent of the owner would not amount to infringement.

Under Article 21A of the Constitutional (86th Amendment) Act of 2002, the right to education was established as a separate fundamental right. All children between the ages of six and fourteen are entitled to a free and obligatory education, according to the article. Article 41 of the Constitution mandates that states adopt adequate plans for providing education, employment, and social assistance within their borders.

The legislature has expressly adopted this under Section 52(1)(i) and Section 52(1)(j), where dealing with copyright material is exempt from copyright infringement. It is stated in the subsections that such acts that are done in good faith for educational purposes will not be considered infringement.

Under Section 52 of the Copyright Act of 1957, there are a few exceptions to copyright infringement. Without the owner's permission, the provision allows for limited use of copyright material.

"52. Certain acts not to be infringement of copyright. —

(1) The following acts shall not constitute an infringement of copyright, namely, —

(a) a fair dealing with any work, not being a computer programme, for the purposes of—

(i) private or personal use, including research;

(i) the reproduction of any work—

(i) by a teacher or a pupil in the course of instruction; or

(ii) as part of the question to be answered in an examination; or

(iii) in answers to such questions;"[1]

In this case, the content present in "Our Mission" has been used by the author for his research paper and therefore, there is no infringement on the part of Mr. Daman Dev Sood as his use is bonafide for research and also, he has given reference of the site.

---

[1] *Sec 52, Copyrights Act, 1957 available at -* MergedFile (copyright.gov.in)

7. Case6: BCI BCM Lifecycle Diagram

While developing my new/ recent course on Operational Resilience, I wanted to make use of the BCM Lifecycle diagram (the geared wheel diagram) created by the BCI. I wrote to them:

"I am developing a course on Operational Resilience where I have a reference to BCM and would like to use the below diagram: (not showing now due to their response – see below).

I will say that it is from BCI (www.thebci.org) or I can use any text that you suggest. Please let me know if any reservations or the suggestive text."

I was sure that it was in public domain and there won't be any challenges, but the response was different:

"Unfortunately, as a rule we do not allow use of the Lifecycle for commercial activities which it sounds like this is for a course."

The response was from **Head of Commercial.**

So, with thanks, I created my own diagram as below (I hope there is no copyright on the terms used by me, but I will be happy to be challenged, for knowledge enhancement:

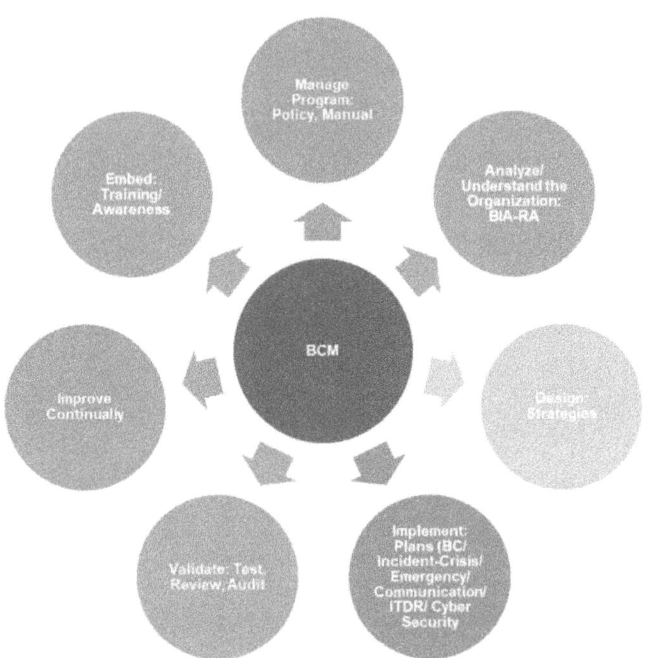

8. Case7: Aveva Group Paper

This interaction with Aveva group.

"I have downloaded 'Whitepaper_ARC_Operational-Excellence-OpX-Achieved-by-Companies-That-ARE-Operationally-Resilient_EN' from your website after providing my details as required.

I am developing a course on Operational Resilience and would like to make use of it:

1) I would like to share this document with my participants – I will not make any changes – exact document will be shared.
2) I would like to make use of the diagrams in the document and some commentary in my courseware.

Do you have any reservations? Please let me know."

And the response (was not easy to get the response though, unlike all above cases so far):

"Hello Daman,

Please find the details below for the usage of the document.

26

"You may use the full unmodified document for the class. For the diagrams, we would only ask that you provide attribution for them in your course work. Such as simply citing ARC Research as the source for the first two diagrams and AVEVA for the third."

Hope this helps.

"

I will do accordingly now in my next course i.e. Operational Resilience Professional Course.

9. Case8: Google Search for Images

I search for 'free BCM images' on google and get the following output:

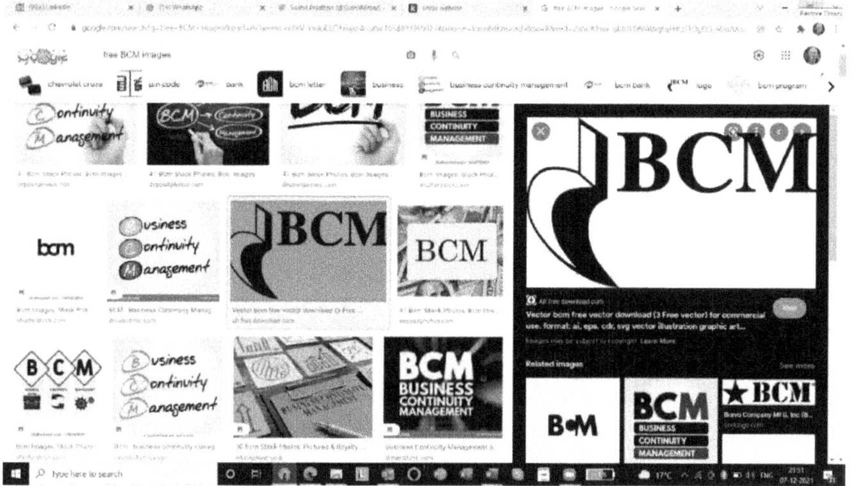

I download this by right clicking and use it in my courseware.

There is no reference to the source in my courseware.

Am in infringing any rule/ regulation/ act?

If I change the colours in this image – does that become my product/ copyright? I am told even if you make minutest changes – that becomes your baby.

Commentary:

I. THE WORK

In the current scenario, we can see a website providing free logos for commercial use. Before downloading the picture and using it with our content, we need to ensure that it fulfils certain criteria:

1. **Creative work of supplier/provider**
   We need to ensure that the website providing such free logos, literary information, etc. are themselves authorized or the owner of the work. It shall be original work and legally authorized as per their disposal.

2. **Consent:**
   a. **Creator/author/owner to supplier/provider**

To ensure the legitimacy of product being used by third parties, the supplier/provider should have obtained consent from rightful owner, in case if he is not the owner. In the current scenario, we can see all-free-donwload.com providing BCM image. If the image doesn't belong to them or they are not the original creator of the work, then they should have consent of owner.

b. **Creator/author/owner/supplier to user**

Where the creative work is not free for use and comes with a certain price tag, then it is completely illegal to use, it without paying for the same. On the other hand, where there is no price mentioned, but it is silent of being used for commercial use or no express permission is provided; still it is illegal to use, provided owner has consented for the same.

c. **Piracy**

Sufficient measures and research shall be taken as a man of ordinary prudence to ensure that the product is not pirated or that no similar product of the same resemblance, quality, proximity, and substantial quality is available somewhere else. For example: One may download a pirated movie with the help of torrent or other like applications. However, very few are aware that under provisions of Cinematograph Act of 2019, if a person knowingly downloads copyrighted movie, it can result into jail along with hefty fine. Hence, user shall perform necessary precaution.

II.   USE AND COPYRIGHT

Where the above criteria mentioned under point I are checked and complied with, next comes the question whether the use of such work, along with our copyright work, makes us owner of the picture as well?

To understand the answer, first, the attention is drawn to the following provision:

Section 17 of the *Copyright Act, 1957*[2], states, " *Subject to the provisions of this Act, the author of a work shall be the first owner of the copyright therein: (a) In the case of a literary, dramatic or artistic work made by the author in the course of his employment by the proprietor of a newspaper, magazine or*

---

[2] *Sec 17, Copyrights Act, 1957 available at -* <u>MergedFile (copyright.gov.in)</u>

similar periodical under a contract of service or apprenticeship, for the purpose of publication in a newspaper, magazine or similar periodical, the said proprietor shall, in the absence of any agreement to the contrary, be the first owner of the copyright in the work in so far as the copyright relates to the publication of the work in any newspaper, magazine or similar periodical, or to the reproduction of the work for the purpose of its being so published, but in all other respects the author shall be the first owner of the copyright in the work;"

Therefore, in the current scenario and provision of law, following conclusions can be drawn:

1. We are not the authors of the original work/image;
2. It is created and provided by a third-party entity, and we are not empowered to prohibit a third party from supplying the similar image to any other party.

Hence, use to such image even in our original copyrighted literary work, doesn't entitle us to be owner or claim rights over the same.

10. Case9: HBR Articles

I have subscribed to HBR and receive free articles from them. These do not have anything at all about 'copyrights'.

i) Can I share this with others – as it is, in full?

ii) Can I use part/ full of this (with full reference) in my discussions/ writings?

iii) Can I comment upon the contents of this paper – in authoring my paper?

Commentary:

i) Yes, you can share this with others, but the use should not be commercial in nature. You cannot sell it, but you can share it for research/education purpose. Making money out of someone else's work isn't permitted but using it for educating comes under fair use of the content.

This has been officially enacted by the legislature under Sections 52(1)(i) and 52(1)(j), which deal with copyright work as an exception to copyright infringement. It is stated in the subsections that certain acts will not be considered infringement if they are carried out in good faith for educational purposes.

As per section 52 of Copyrights Act,[3]

(a) *a fair dealing with any work, not being a computer programme, for the purposes of—*

(i) *private or personal use, including research;*

ii)   Yes, it can be used with proper referencing.

iii)   Yes, you can comment on the contents of the paper and since it will be your own writing, there's no violation.

---

[3] *Sec 52, Copyrights Act, 1957 available at -* <u>*MergedFile (copyright.gov.in)*</u>

11. Case10: Australian Government Tool

I downloaded the following tool from https://www.organisationalresilience.gov.au/HealthCheck/instructions# (no restrictions, no copyright information)

I use this in my copyrighted course (I did not include this tool in my copyright application) with full reference to the source.

Am in infringement of any rule/ regulation/ act?

Commentary:

In the present case, the user is downloading tool from a government site which meane the information is already in public domain.

The term "public domain" refers to creative works that are not copyrighted, allowing anybody to use them in any way they want (while crediting the source or author of the work), including reselling or using the material to produce new or updated versions without the owners' permission or compensation.

There is no violation of any rule or regulation as the tool that is downloaded is in public domain and can be accessed freely by anyone.

12. Case11: My Copyrighted Courses

I run many courses. One of them is Certified Organisational Resilience Specialist Course, copyrighted to me. I share the courseware with the participants who are paying for the course. The courseware shows the copyright information clearly and also the following text

"**NOTE TO READERS**

The following work is registered as a Copyright Work with the Government of India. This work is prohibited to be used as Creative Commons or with acknowledgement. Hence, you are requested to kindly refrain from illegal practices involving reproduction, copy, forward, disclose, publish, sale, display, trade or use any part of the copyright protected work. Otherwise, you will attract penal provisions of legal proceedings. "

I also write to them that the courseware is for their use only and cannot be shared with anyone else in any form.

What are the participants' rights on this courseware? What if they share it with someone else? Can they print it (I share the softcopies only – currently the courses are in online mode. But during offline/ in person deliveries, the printed copies of the courseware are shared with the participants)?

Commentary:

In this case, the courseware is shared with the participants by the author.

If participants use it (share it) with people just to educate them then there is no Violation as per sec 52 of the act, but if they try to sell it or make some monetary gain, then they will be violating the author's rights.

As far as printing is concerned, yes, the participants can print once they get courseware from the author but how they are using it is the question of concern. If the use is for any of the act mentioned under section 52 as an exceptional case where the act will not constitute infringement, then printing is fine but if it is for any other purpose, then printing and distributing will constitute infringement and may attract punishment (both imprisonment and fine).

13. Case12: ISO Standard

Someone purchased a standard from ISO. The document has this stamp:

i)   Can this be printed?

ii)   Can this be shared with colleagues in the same organisation?

What infringement will be made, if any? Any copyrights violations?

Commentary:

Without the explicit consent of the copyright owners, a fair deal for research, study, criticism, review, and news reporting is authorised, as well as the use of works in libraries, schools, and legislatures. Exemptions have been prescribed in respect of various uses of copyrighted works in order to protect the interests of users.

Thus, it can be printed and shared with colleagues, but no commercial use is permitted. It can be printed and used for any of the acts mentioned under Section 52.

14. Case13: Copyright-101_Handbook

I received a 'Copyright-101_Handbook' as forwarded message on a whatsapp group called 'ERM Professionals'.

i) Is it ok on part of that person to share it?

ii) Is it ok for me to download and save on my machine?

iii) Is it ok for me to make use of it in this paper?

iv) Can I read and benefit from the information in the book?

Commentary:

In the present case, the objective of ERM Professionals' group is to share knowledge with other professionals of the same field so it is completely fine on the part of that person to share it with his fellow professionals for the sake of knowledge enhancement.

Since the handbook is shared for educational purpose which comes under the exceptions mentioned under section 52 of the Copyrights Act, downloading, and saving it doesn't amount to any kind of infringement.

As per section 52 of Copyrights Act, [4]

a fair dealing with any work, not being a computer programme, for the purposes of—

(i) private or personal use, including research

However, if you want to use it in research paper, proper referencing should be done in order to make readers aware about the source of information.

Reading it and benefiting from the information available in the handbook is not punishable and cab be done without any hesitation!

---

[4] *Sec 52, Copyrights Act, 1957 available at -* <u>*MergedFile (copyright.gov.in)*</u>

15. Case14: McKinsey Reports - Documents

I have subscribed to McKinsey, and I receive many documents/ reports from them that have various options like:

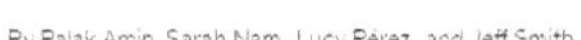

By Palak Amin, Sarah Nam, Lucy Pérez, and Jeff Smith

Biopharma companies should consider a new, integrated approach to evidence-generation strategies to better demonstrate the value of

At the bottom is a copyright information also:

-biopharma-final.pdf - Adobe Acrobat Reader DC (64-bit)

Palak Amin is a consultant in McKinsey's Philadelphia office; **Sarah Nam** is an associate partner in the Washington, DC, office; and **Lucy Pérez** is a senior partner in the Boston office, where **Jeff Smith** is a partner.

The authors wish to thank David Champagne, Alex Davidson, Mattias Evers, Tomoko Nagatani, Brandon Parry, Lydia The, and Jan van Overbeeke for their contributions to this article.

i)   Can I download and store this on my computer?

ii)   Can I share this with others?

iii)   I am authoring my next book where I pick up the subject from this report (with full reference to the report), some content and write some commentary of my own on top of that. It is clear what is from the McKinsey report and what is my writing.

Am I in infringement of any rule/ regulation/ act?

Commentary:

Yes, since you've subscribed to McKinsey, you'll receive updates from them and downloading and saving it is not an offence. As far as sharing is concerned, section 52 gives you the benefit of fairly using it.

And in the book that you are authoring, using the content with proper references will not make the content plagiarised and it will not amount to the violation of any kind of rule/regulation.

46

16. Case15: IEEE Magazines

I am a member of IEEE (www.ieee.org) on paid membership basis. My subscription includes access to the monthly magazines from them. I receive this from IEEE with an option to read it online or download. I download this every time.

What are my rights with respect to the usage of this magazine?

Commentary:

Sometimes, we are provided content, questionnaires, literary work, or course material for being members of any organization, committee, etc. This may be issued to us either annually or half-yearly or quarterly. This work is provided to us at our disposal; however, it must be clearly noted that we are not the author of the original work. It is the source from which we are subscribed, who are the originator and author of original literary work.

Despite payment of subscription fee, we are not the owner of the same and have no exclusive rights. However, Section 52 of the Copyright Act, 1957, confer certain rights on us as being designated receivers. These rights include:

1. Make private/personal use for research;
2. Criticism or review of that work;
3. Reporting of current events and current affairs;
4. Make back-up copies purely as protection against loss, destruction, or damage in order to utilize for the purpose for which it was supplied;
5. Observation and study of the material;
6. Make copies and adaptation for a legally obtained copy for non-commercial personal use;
7. Reproduction of any work for purpose of judicial proceeding or for purpose of report of judicial proceedings;
8. Reproduction of publication of any work prepared by the secretariat of a legislature or when the legislature consists of two houses, by the secretariat of either house of the legislature, exclusively for the use of the members of that legislature;

9. Reproduction of any work in certified copy made or supplied in accordance with any law for the time being in force;

10. Reading and reciting in public of reasonable extracts from a publishing literary work;

11. The performance, in the course of the activities of an educational institution, of a literary, dramatic, or musical work by the staff and students of the institution, or of a cinematograph film or a sound recording if the audience is limited to such staff and students, the parents and guardians of the students and persons connected with the activities of the institution or the communication to such an audience of a cinematograph film or sound recording;

12. The performance of a literary, dramatic, or musical work by an amateur club or society, if the performance is given to a non-paying audience, or for the benefit of a religious institution;

13. The reproduction in a newspaper, magazine, or other periodical of an article on current economic, political, social, or religious topics,

unless the author of such article has expressly reserved to himself the right of such reproduction;

14. The storing of a work in any medium by electronic means by a non-commercial public library, for preservation if the library already possesses a non-digital copy of the work;

15. The making of not more than three copies of a book (including a pamphlet, sheet of music, map, chart, or plan) by or under the direction of the person in charge of a non-commercial public library for the use of the library if such book is not available for sale in India;

16. The reproduction, for the purpose of research or private study or with a view to publication, of an unpublished literary, dramatic, or musical work kept in a library, museum, or other institution to which the public has access;

17. The making or publishing of a painting, drawing, engraving or photograph of a work of architecture or the display of a work of architecture;

18. the use by the author of an artistic work, where the author of such work is not the owner of the

copyright therein, of any mould, cast, sketch, plan, model, or study made by him for the purpose of the work: Provided that he does not thereby repeat or imitate the main design of the work;

19. The making of an ephemeral recording, by a broadcasting organisation using its own facilities for its own broadcast by a broadcasting organisation of a work which it has the right to broadcast; and the retention of such recording for archival purposes on the ground of its exceptional documentary character;

20. The performance of a literary, dramatic, or musical work or the communication to the public of such work or of a sound recording in the course of any bona fide religious ceremony or an official ceremony held by the Central Government or the State Government or any local authority;

21. The reconstruction of a building or structure in accordance with the architectural drawings or plans by reference to which the building or structure was originally constructed: Provided that the original construction was made with the

consent or licence of the owner of the copyright in such drawings and plans;

22. The production or publication of a translation in any Indian language of an Act of a Legislature and of any rules or orders made thereunder-

a) If no translation of such Act or rules or orders in that language has previously been produced or published by the Government; or

b) Where a translation of such Act or rules or orders in that language has been produced or published by the Government, if the translation is not available for sale to the public: Provided that such translation contains a statement at a prominent place to the effect that the translation has not been authorised or accepted as authentic by the Government;

23. The reproduction or publication of-

a) any matter which has been published in any Official Gazette except an Act of a Legislature;

b) any Act of a Legislature subject to the condition that such Act is reproduced or published together with any commentary thereon or any other original matter;

c) the report of any committee, commission, council, board, or other like body appointed by the Government if such report has been laid on the Table of the Legislature, unless the reproduction or publication of such report is prohibited by the Government;

d) any judgment or order of a court, tribunal, or other judicial authority, unless the reproduction or publication of such judgment or order is prohibited by the court, the tribunal or other judicial authority, as the case may be;

24. The inclusion in a cinematograph film of-

a) Any artistic work permanently situates in a public place or any premises to which the public has access; or

b) Any other artistic work, if such inclusion is only by way of background or is otherwise incidental to the principal matters represented in the film;

25. The adaptation, reproduction, issue of copies or communication to the public of any work in any accessible format, by-

a) Any person to facilitate persons with disability to access to works including sharing with any person with disability of such accessible format for private or personal use, educational purpose, or research; or

b) Any organisation working for the benefit of the persons with disabilities in case the normal format prevents the enjoyment of such works by such persons;

26. The causing of a recording to be heard in public by utilizing it-

a) In an enclosed room or hall meant for the common use of residents in any residential premises (not being a hotel or similar commercial establishment) as part of the amenities provided exclusively or mainly for residents therein; or

b) As part of the activities of a club or similar organisation which is not established or conducted for profit;

27. the importation of copies of any literary or artistic work, such as labels, company logos or promotional or explanatory material, that is purely incidental to other goods or products being imported lawfully;

28. Reproduction of any work-

a) By a teacher or a pupil in course of instruction; or

b) As part of the question to be answered in an examination; or

c) In answers to any such questions.

Therefore, as it well observed under the law, supplied by the original work does not make us joint owners of the same, however, we are provided with the above rights to ensure adequate usage and enjoyment of the work.

17. Case16: Documents Created While in Employment

Person A was working at XYZ company and created/ received many documents/ presentations/ reports. He also had access to some contacts internal-as well-external. He had signed NDA with XYZ company. He then moved to PQR company and carried some of these – reports, contacts, documents, presentation with him without the knowledge of XYZ company.

i)   Is A in infringement of any rule/ regulation/ act? Legal/ ethical?

      A, while working with PQR company, refers to these while creating content for PQR?

      A, while working with PQR company, makes use of some of the information from these artefacts?

ii)   Is A in infringement with any rule/ regulations/act?

iii)   Or do you believe that this case is beyond the broader scope of this paper i.e. IPR/ Copyrights etc.?

Commentary:

Before analysing the situation portrayed, first we need to understand following concepts of law:

I. Under Section 17(c) the Copyright Act, 1957 in case the work was made in course of author's employment under a contract of service or apprenticeship, the employer shall be the first owner of copyright therein. Such works may be created in various capacities such as:

1. **Freelancer/Commissioned work**

    Such work is where the person is hired for a certain commission or remuneration for a particular task or assignment or project. The person hired fulfilled the duty or role cast upon him as per agreement and post which he is paid for his services. Any such work performed or created on demand and for hirer, makes him the author of the same.

2.   Contract of Employment

Under contract of employment, the employer hires a person, for performing certain work. This contract may be contract of service and for service. Contract of service refers to a contract where the manner of executing performance is specified by the employer. On the other hand, in a contact for service, the employee is told to perform his skills as per his knowledge to execute the work assigned to him without express instructions from the employer. In both the situations, the employee's rights as original author are relinquished. The copyright protection is extended to the employer under whose command the work was created. Common examples can be found around us such as news reporting, news articles, etc.

II.   In the current situation, we can also observe that reference has been drawn to Non-Disclosure Agreement. A non-disclosure agreement is an agreement between an employer and employee that established confidential relationship between them regarding any work or task performed during course of employment. This is executed between the parties to protect sensitive trade secrets or information that would provide unfair advantage to other company at the cost of loss of originating company.

The Non-disclosure agreement may be in the form of a clause in contract of employment or separate agreement. The employee whether during the tenure of employment or post the termination of employment is bound by the agreement. In any circumstance, if the employee breaches the agreement, the employer can seek compensation in the form of damages from him. The damages may be liquidated or non-liquidated as agreed between the parties.

Now coming on the situation presented and legal principles, inference can be drawn, that while working with PQR company, if A makes use of information or literary work created under employment of XYZ company, he will be guilty of infringement of copyright under Section 51 of the Copyright Act, 1957. This section pertains to unauthorized use without consent, license or assignment by the owner that hampers his exclusive rights over work. A can be prosecuted under the following provision of law:

1. For breaching non-disclosure agreement:

Section 73 of Indian Contract Act, 1872, which states:

"When a contract has been broken, the party who suffers by such breach is entitled to receive, from the party who has broken the contract, compensation for any loss or damage caused to him thereby, which naturally arose in the usual course of things from such breach, or which the parties knew, when they made the contract, to be likely to result from the breach of it."[5]

---

[5] *Sec 73, The Indian Contract Act 1872 available at - A1872-09.pdf (legislative.gov.in)*

2.   For disclosing copyright protected work of previous employer:

Section 63 of the Copyright Act, 1957, which states:
"Any person who knowingly infringes or abets the infringement of the copyrighted work shall be punishable with imprisonment for a term which shall not be less than six months, but which may extend to three years and with fine which shall not be less than fifty thousand rupees, but which may extend to two lakh rupees."6

Hence, any such disclosure of information done by A will make him guilty of copyright infringement as well breaching contract.

---

6 *Section 63, Copyrights Act, 1957 available at* <u>MergedFile (copyright.gov.in)</u>

18. Case17: ORCG Interim Guidance

I downloaded 'ORCG Interim Guidance for Firm Operational Resilience' available through a linkedin post. Once again wanted to be sure before usage and sharing.

"I have downloaded this. Can I share with my contacts (no change by me – just as downloaded)?"

And I am happy with the response:

"Hi Daman, thanks for asking. As its TLP White it means it can be shared publicly so feel free to share amongst your contacts."

I have not received further response on asking what TLP White is and whether I can share as additional reading material with my course participants also, but I am taking it easy and will share.

Later I could find here <u>Traffic Light Protocol (TLP) Definitions and Usage | CISA</u> [7] and happy to reproduce a portion:

Color	When should it be used?	How may it be shared?
TLP:RED Not for disclosure, restricted to participants only.	Sources may use TLP:RED when information cannot be effectively acted upon by additional parties, and could lead to impacts on a party's privacy, reputation, or operations if misused.	Recipients may not share TLP:RED information with any parties outside of the specific exchange, meeting, or conversation in which it was originally disclosed. In the context of a meeting, for example, TLP:RED information is limited to those present at the meeting. In most circumstances, TLP:RED should be exchanged verbally or in person.
TLP:AMBER Limited disclosure, restricted to participants' organizations.	Sources may use TLP:AMBER when information requires support to be effectively acted upon, yet carries risks to privacy, reputation, or operations if shared outside of the organizations involved.	Recipients may only share TLP:AMBER information with members of their own organization, and with clients or customers who need to know the information to protect themselves or prevent further harm. **Sources are at liberty to specify additional intended limits of the sharing: these must be adhered to.**
TLP:GREEN Limited disclosure, restricted to the community.	Sources may use TLP:GREEN when information is useful for the awareness of all participating organizations as well as with peers within the broader community or sector.	Recipients may share TLP:GREEN information with peers and partner organizations within their sector or community, but not via publicly accessible channels. Information in this category can be circulated widely within a particular community. TLP:GREEN information may not be released outside of the community.
TLP:WHITE Disclosure is not limited.	Sources may use TLP:WHITE when information carries minimal or no foreseeable risk of misuse, in accordance with applicable rules and procedures for public release.	Subject to standard copyright rules, TLP:WHITE information may be distributed without restriction.

---

[7] *Traffic Light Protocol (TLP) Definitions and Usage | CISA*

19. Case18: BCI Document

I am a member of BCI, got a mail from them about a new document released by them and I had the right to download (all clear so far) so I have downloaded (the document is on my machine now).

The copyright notice in the book says '..no part of this publication may be reproduced, stored in a retrieval system...' – so am I making a mistake by storing on my machine that is backup up on a regular basis, and I may make multiple copies of backup also?

I am writing to BCI also.

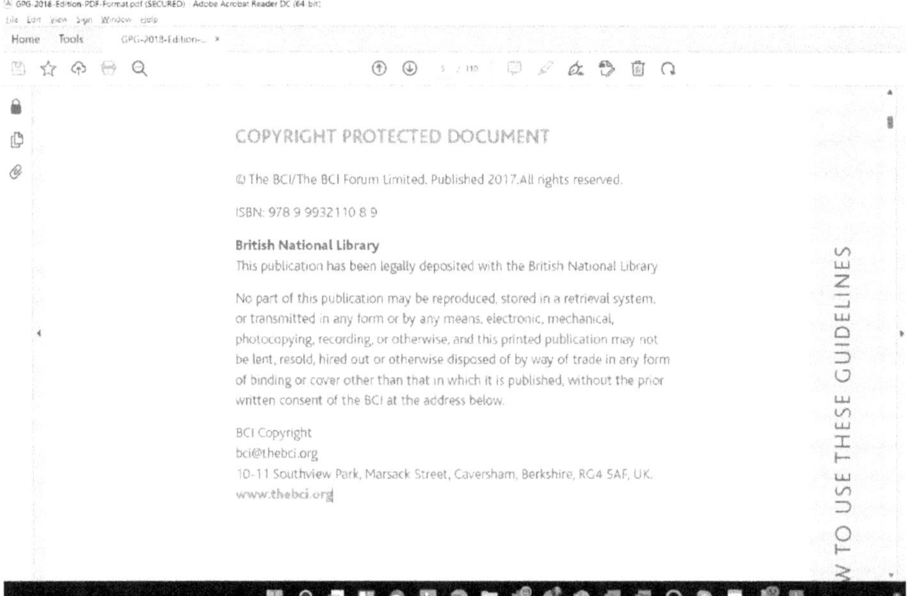

Commentary:

The document itself says that "No part of this publication may be reproduced, stored in a retrieval system, or transmitted in any form or by any means electronic, mechanical, photocopying recording or otherwise and this printed publication may not by lent, resold, hired out or otherwise disposed of by way of trade in any form of binding or cover other than that in which it is published without the prior written consent of the BCI as the address below."
As per my understanding, since you are a member of BCI and they themselves informed you about the release of the new document by them thereby giving you all the permissions to download the document, there should be no infringement on your part in downloading and saving it.

However, the document should be dealt fairly, as per section 52 of the Copyrights Act. If you use it in an unfair manner (and try to make profit out of it by making copies and distributing them) then you can be charged for infringement, but, till the time the intention of use is bona fide, I don't think any legal consequences may arise.

66

20. Case19: A Document by Mohit Mangal

Someone shared the attached document in a whatsapp group. The document appeared to be useful and has info; but I wanted to be sure w.r.t copyrights infringements. Asked the sender to clarify, but as usual people share blindly and do not respond to any queries – he/ she didn't.

So, I wrote to the author. And here is the response:

"Dear Mr. Daman Sood,

Thanks for connecting with me regarding 'Parents' Handbook of Careers after School'.

Yes, you can forward it to others.

If you wish to Donate anything to my foundation, please feel free and contribute. Details are there on page 59 of the book. Kindly encourage others also to contribute so that we can get more such publications in future.

Warm Regards-Mohit Mangal"

I hope, I can now safely share this with all.

Commentary:

Since the handbook is shared for educational
purpose which comes under the exceptions
mentioned under section 52 of the Copyrights Act,
downloading, and saving it doesn't amount to any
kind of infringement.

21. Case20: ISACA Risk Starter Kit

A professional colleague wrote in a WhatsApp group "ISACA has developed Risk Starter Kit to help risk managers. You can find it here: (and the link was given).

It is free for members. Is it possible for you to share? I am not the member now."

    a. Did this person break any law in asking the 'members only document'?

I wrote after few days "hope you got response to this. Please share with me also, part of my research, I want to see how a members only document can be shared."

This person did not respond, but another professional from the group wrote to me one-on-one "I shared the document with the first member. Will share it with you also."

I just asked whether he was an ISACA member, and he responded 'yes. No provision to share member-only document but just out of goodwill and help to each other." And he shared the same with me also. I have not opened it yet.

    a. Did he breach any copyrights in sharing with others?

b. Would I breach any copyright if I open and use it?
c. Would I be in non-compliance to any provisions if I share it further with other people?

Commentary:

Yes, asking for a members only document is ethically and legally wrong. However, if the member is sharing the document with some of his colleagues for knowledge sharing, it will come under the ambit of fair use and since you've received this document for enhancing knowledge about a particular thing, opening and reading it will not amount to any breach/infringement on your part.

Further sharing of this document will not be a violation of any rule if the purpose of sharing is non-commercial in nature and is in consonance with section 52 of the Copyrights Act 1957.

Anchita Sood

Executive – Membership and Program,

Indian Institute of Insolvency Professionals of ICAI,

Noida *

Daman Dev Sood, FBCI, FBCS, CBCI, SMIEEE, MAIMA, M.IOD, ISO 22301 LA & Expert

IEEE Ambassador

Chair – CS Chapter, IEEE Delhi Section

Member Champion – IEEE India MOVE Partner Relations Committee

IEEE Computer Society Distinguished Contributor (Inaugural Class)

Program Director – Operational Resilience, EY *

International Resilience Trainer & Consultant

Reskube Partner

Email: dbdsood@hotmail.com

Phone: +91 9958091880 (whatsapp)

https://www.damandevsood.com/

https://youtube.com/damandevsood

https://www.linkedin.com/in/damandevsood/

https://www.facebook.com/dbdsood

https://twitter.com/DamanDevSood

https://www.instagram.com/damandevsood/

https://medium.com/@damandevsood

https://in.pinterest.com/damandevsood

Author of "My Experiments With BCM" available at notionpress.com, amazon.in, amazon.co.uk, amazon.com, flipkart.com, kriso.it, wob.com, barnesandnoble.com, ebook.de, books.google.co.in, fnac.com, bookdepository.com , shop.wordbookstores.com, fnac.pt, kizzybooksandmore.com

Author of the "Step by Step guide to the NCEMA 7000: Implement BCM the UAE way" - Available online at the Kindle store

* views presented are authors' own and do not represent their organizations in any way